THE ARABIAN HORSE OF EGYPT

THE ARABIAN HORSE OF EGYPT

Photographs by
Nasr Marei

Foreword by
HRH Princess Alia Bint Al Hussein

Introduction by
Cynthia Culbertson

The American University in Cairo Press
Cairo   New York

To my father, Sayed Marei, and my mother, Soad Marei,
with great love and appreciation. My father gave me the
legacy of the horse and ideals to emulate in my life, and my
mother, the love of life and respect for all living beings.
To my sister, Amina, who loved and cherished horses and
left us too soon.

First published in paperback in 2014 by
The American University in Cairo Press
113 Sharia Kasr el Aini, Cairo, Egypt
420 Fifth Avenue, New York, NY 10018
www.aucpress.com

Dar el Kutub No. 23471/13
ISBN 978 977 416 665 5

Dar el Kutub Cataloging-in-Publication Data

Marei, Nasr
          The Arabian Horse of Egypt / Nasr Marei.—Cairo: The American
    University in Cairo Press, 2014
              p.   cm.
              ISBN 978 977 416 665 5
              1. Arabian horse—Egypt   I. Title
              636.112

1 2 3 4 5 6   18 17 16 15 14

Designed by Andrea El-Akshar
Printed in China

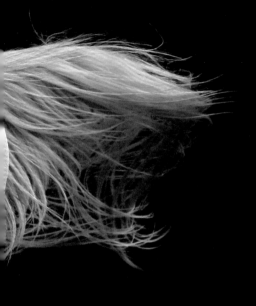

CONTENTS

ACKNOWLEDGMENTS

I would like to thank my brother, Hassan Marei, for his support and encouragement through the years. For their contributions to this book, my deepest appreciation goes to HRH Princess Alia Bint Al Hussein of Jordan, Cynthia Culbertson, and Abu Bakr El Kot, who all share my love of the Egyptian horse. Together we brought this book to fruition.

I would also like to thank Pat Canfield for her editorial contribution.

Since this book is a celebration of the Egyptian Arabian horse in general, the names of the horses captured in the photographs and their breeders were purposely left out. I would like, however, to thank the following stud farms for granting permission to use photographs of their horses: Al Farida, Al Mamlaka, Ariela, Simeon, Prestige, Trebazane, and of course, Albadeia.

FOREWORD

HRH Princess Alia Bint Al Hussein

I am honored to be given the opportunity to write a few words of introduction to this beautiful book.

The artist behind the photographs, however, needs no introduction. Nasr is well known in several fields. His father, the late Sayed Marei, was largely responsible for ensuring the continuation of the Arabian horse in Egypt during a critical period in Egypt's history, and remained a strong influence behind the Egyptian Agricultural Organization's (EAO) Stud Farm of El Zahraa while founding his own stud, Albadeia.

Nasr has thus known horses all his life. However, his special sensitivity and eye are qualities which cannot be learned; he has proved to be not only a sound (and therefore very popular) Arabian-horse judge, but has bred some wonderful horses himself. He continues to select fresh blood, or outcrosses for his stock, in a way which shows objectivity and vision, qualities which are, in truth, not common in the highly emotive world of the Arabian horse.

In addition, and as is clearly demonstrated in the following pages, Nasr is a talented photographer. His sincere appreciation of the essential qualities of his subjects—beauty, free spirit, intelligence, and humor—is underlined here by the manner in which he has chosen to portray them: at rest, at play, and expressing themselves as only the unique Arabian horse can.

The text by Cynthia Culbertson provides a rich overview of the history of these fascinating creatures. The Arabian horse has a special place in the tradition of the Arab people. It is referred to in many sayings of the Prophet, one being, "if your neighbor owns a horse but you do not, open a window in the wall between you so that its blessings can still reach you."

Amir Abd al-Qadir, the Algerian warrior and mystic, refers to horses as "comets" that protect from demons, and many people can attest to the way in which horses seem to dispel negative energy

A valuable lesson may be learned from the tale of Shu'ayb bin al-Hajjaj, who was compiling a book of the Prophet's sayings. He refused to visit a certain person who was reputed to know of such a saying, because he had heard that that person caught his horse by pretending to offer it tidbits. Anyone who would lie to a horse, he felt, was capable of lying about the Prophet himself, and could not therefore be trusted!

This volume provides a tantalizing taste of the magic that is the Arabian horse. I hope that this will be the first of many books by Nasr, and I salute him for his contributions to the horse world, for his sterling qualities as a human being, and for being a good friend.

PREFACE

Nasr Marei

When I think of the Arabian horse it is often with the inner eye of an artist. It is an image of great beauty, free spirit, elegant flowing movement, and proud character. I have been blessed to have been born into a family with a thriving farm in the verdant Delta of Egypt just north of Cairo. Horses were always a part of our life so that it was not unusual for me to wander into one of the horse stalls with my breakfast when I was four years old. The sight and sounds of the horse have always been part of my life. This initial interest blossomed through the years into a full-blown love of the horse.

In 1935, my grandfather bought our first Arabian fillies from the Royal Agricultural Society, later the Egyptian Agricultural Organization (EAO), and established the Albadeia breeding program which I carry on to this day. Being born and raised among horses, I found many possibilities opened up as I learned more about them and learned to love them. It is truly a never-ending involvement and passion, since one constantly evolves through experience, additional knowledge and an appreciation of the artistry and at the same time, the functionality that culminate in the Arabian horse. The challenge is to better oneself while bettering the world for the horse. Reading, traveling, and judging in Arabian horse shows throughout the world continues to widen my vision of what is possible. It helps to keep me open-minded about different approaches to understanding the horse.

At my stud farm we have a gene pool of seventy-five years that is based on our original foundation horses and the breeding of over five hundred horses to date. Even with this strong base, I occasionally will selectively introduce outside elements with a mare or stallion from another breeding program. I do this in the belief that I am doing something that will maintain the 'classic' type and correctness of our horses while adding something that will bring improvement in an area that needs attention, such as stronger movement. It takes objectivity to recognize not only the strong points of your horses but also the aspects that require improvement. An important lesson in this is to attempt to preserve the identity and integrity of your lines without falling victim to the extremes of fashion sometimes seen in the competitive world.

Initially, my father, Sayed Marei, was responsible for building the reputation of Albadeia throughout the world. Gradually my brother Hassan and I joined in the day-to-day operation of the stud. Eventually, I assumed full management of the farm with all the joys and heartbreak that it entails. There are few experiences more wonderful than the birth of a foal or more devastating than the loss of a horse gone before its time; it always seems to be before its time. In the mid-1990s, I retired from the academic and business worlds and devoted myself completely to what is the overriding center of my existence: breeding and living with, and for, the Arabian horse.

When I was younger we were able to ride the half-kilometer from our farm and gallop through the desert at the foot of the Great Pyramids. Today, the urbanization of Greater Cairo has encroached into our world and devoured the surrounding green spaces. I strongly believe that I am carrying the heritage of our ancient civilization into the legacy of my horses. I have tried to create an environment for them that is as close to a natural oasis as possible. My horses live in an ambience of lush flowering gardens, date palm trees, deep sand paddocks, and open stalls. I have tried to allow their existence to carry on without intrusion from the outside chaos. My lifestyle is such that I have made the horses my family and have attempted to create the best possible world for us where they can thrive, and I can be part of their daily lives.

A large number of variables factor into any intelligent breeding decision. One of the key issues is to study the history and origin of the Arabian horse. You cannot separate its history from your decisions. The Arabian horse is an example of survival in the harshest of environments. The desert often engendered romantic fantasies in early travelers. However, the reality is far from that; it is harsh and unforgiving. Only the strongest of body as well as courage and spirit could survive. This is what gives today's Arabian its special characteristics. If you breed these qualities out of the horse, it loses what makes it unique. As in architecture and design, form does follow function. I illustrate these characteristics in my selection of photographs.

I am fortunate to have over fifty years of breeding experience, which allows me to recognize traits and genetic potential to draw on in making my decisions. Like any serious breeder, I know what the individual pedigrees mean in so far as which characteristics are dominant and where problems might arise. I am able to access not only the pedigrees of the horses I have bred, but also the ancestors of the foundation horses from the EAO and the Royal Family studs. This helps me to predict the outcome of breeding a specific mare and stallion. In this way I can try to preserve the look that we have established in our program through the years while introducing bloodlines that can add the elements I feel are important.

When making the breeding selections, it is important to include disposition as an element because some bloodlines and individual horses have marked characteristics that you want to preserve or eliminate. Charisma, too, is dominant in certain lines. An important thing to remember is that the 'classic' horse, which embodies these traits, along with balance and symmetry, is timeless, whereas the fashion of the day has little staying power. I try to regard myself as someone who is continuing the legacy of horse breeding as a guardian of centuries-old traditions.

Painting, sculpture, and literature, especially poetry, abound with images of the Bedouin warhorse. Studying these works gives today's breeder a sense of the courage and intelligence that were demanded of these horses in addition to their tremendous agility and endurance. And yet one sees power and beauty first before the great determination and effort coursing through the horse's body. This struggle for survival created an unbreakable bond between horse and rider and allowed for both to exist together in a world that constantly threatened to destroy them. Although there could be great devotion between the warriors and their mounts, their lives also demanded a break in the attachment with total lack of compassion when necessary.

In my photographs I try to capture some of the essence of these great paintings and lithographs. It is my way to capture the free spirit and charisma of the horse and freeze that instant in time so that I can relive it for years to come. It satisfies my artistic and aesthetic love of the beauty that abounds in nature. Photography has been a long-time passion: ever since my father gave me a Kodak Brownie when I was seven years old. A Nikon camera at the age of eleven cemented my desire to photograph anything that I felt was beautiful in nature, landscapes, and of course, horses. Underwater scenes and desert landscapes are part of what I continue to photograph today. Clearly my equipment has improved drastically since the early days.

However, it has always been the horse that is at the core of my photography. Because of my years of experience with the horse, I am able to anticipate the movement and capture the essence of who I feel that horse to be. I try to capture the elegance, pride, and majesty of each horse, whether it is a mare or stallion, a foal, or a young horse feeling its power begin to explode in movement. As you look at the photographs, be sure to look carefully at the intelligence and curiosity in the expressions of the horses: their soft liquid eyes, flaring nostrils, flagging tails, and almost ethereal movements.

Even after so many years, I continue to strive to preserve and improve the Arabian horse, which I love so much. I want to breed a horse that captures your mind and heart. I want there to be a vision that can trigger your imagination to see yourself riding that horse across a great expanse of rolling desert, with the winds blowing past as your horse's hooves fly across the sands. I want your experience of seeing that horse to take your breath away. Then you will feel some of the love and passion as well as the great respect I have felt through my years with the Arabian horse. They have been my companions and my friends.

To me, the Arabian horse is a gift that we have received from the past and one that we must preserve and bequeath to the future. It is a gift and legacy that we must respect and treasure.

This book is dedicated to the pure Egyptian Arabian horse and all those who feel and enjoy the majesty and magic of who they are, whether in art or in life.

INTRODUCTION

Cynthia Culbertson

To know the Arabian horses of Egypt is to have a unique opportunity to experience a living treasure of the ages. Renowned throughout the world as the finest source of classic Arabian type and pure desert lineage, Egyptian Arabians represent only four percent of the total Arabian horse population yet have an impact far beyond their numbers. To appreciate these magnificent animals fully it is important to understand their fascinating history and significant cultural legacy. Since the horse was introduced into Egypt, it has been associated with the ascendance of power and cultural change. From the age of the pharaohs, the rise of Islam, the dynasties of the Mamluks, to the time of Muhammad Ali, the presence of Arabian horses at decisive historical junctures has helped shape Egyptian history.

The Proto-Arabian

The Arabian horse, considered the world's oldest breed, has been celebrated for its beauty, nobility, and stamina for thousands of years. Yet a veil of mystery shrouds its origins. Most scientists believe a type of horse referred

An Arabian horse—a living work of art.

1

to as the proto-Arabian originated in the Fertile Crescent, where horses were introduced as early as 2300 BCE. Several empires in this region were renowned for their use of the horse and chariot. A cuneiform text of Hittite origin, referred to as the Kikkuli tablets, dates to the fourteenth century BCE and describes the care and training of horses in great detail.[1] Similar training texts were also written by the Assyrians. The horses portrayed in Assyrian and Hittite art, however, are powerful animals whose heavy bodies, thick necks, and sturdy legs bear little resemblance to the future Arabian breed. While archaeological discoveries may yield further clues, the earliest known depictions of the proto-Arabian must be considered critical evidence in solving the mystery of the breed's origins. These depictions—the highly carried heads and tails, arched necks, and delicate limbs distinctive to the modern breed—are first encountered in the art of ancient Egypt.

Pharaoh's Horses

One of the defining characteristics of the ancient Egyptian civilization, which lasted nearly three thousand years, was the ability of the society to prevail with relatively little alteration, but the introduction of the horse and chariot remains one of the most dynamic changes ever embraced by the Egyptians. While the Hyksos, an Asiatic people who invaded Egypt during the Second Intermediate Period (1700–1550 BCE), are often cited as introducing the horse, the exact source of the proto-Arabian is still not proven. It is certain, however, that by harnessing the strength and agility of these horses the Egyptians dramatically enlarged their empire, leaving a legacy of unparalleled cultural achievement.

The Egyptians primarily used stallions in teams of two to pull their chariots for war and the hunt; however, there is the occasional depiction of an Egyptian astride a horse and even one of a messenger appearing to ride bareback and sidesaddle. The Egyptians were perhaps the first to devise an efficient means of transporting horses other than riding or driving them overland. Artwork from the New Kingdom depicts many boats on the Nile carrying horses and their attendants with stalls constructed for the safe transport of this precious cargo. Evidence of horseracing has also been found, and some historians believe the Egyptians were the first to make a true sport of this endeavor.

The proto-Arabians depicted in Egyptian art confirm that these remarkable horses have possessed their unique archetype for thousands of years, and Egyptian literature reveals the high esteem in which the pharaohs held their steeds. In a poem inscribed in five temples, including Karnak, the prolific builder and mighty warrior Ramesses II gave credit for his victory at Kadesh to his horses, even stating the names of this favored team.

And the noble pair of horses that carried
Pharaoh on,
Lo! "Victory of Thebes" was their name.
And from out the royal stables of great
Miamun they came.[2]

The Nubian pharaoh Piye, who was buried with four of his favorite horses, wrote a stirring reprimand to the prince of a town that had met defeat at the hands of the Egyptians. In his letter to the vanquished foe, he wrote, "As I have lived and loved Re and breath is in my nostrils, thus my heart grows heavy seeing how these horses have been starved, which is worse than anything you have done from the evil in your heart."

The Development of the Arabian as a True Breed

Although rock art throughout the Arabian Peninsula and the Middle East features horses with distinctly Arabian silhouettes, most researchers believe the horse was a relatively late import to the Arabian Peninsula, appearing around 300–400 BCE.[3] Despite legends to the contrary, no evidence has yet been found to support the existence of an indigenous equine population, nor does proof exist of a connection between the horses of ancient Egypt and the breed that later developed in Arabia, despite their compelling similarities. What can be proven, however, is that a distinct breed developed in this region that would change the course of equine history.

The characteristics of the Arabian breed point to centuries of adaptation to the desert, and its genetic prepotency is consistent with development in relative geographic isolation. While Arabia's forbidding terrain generally limited external influences to the historical trading routes along the boundaries of the peninsula, the interior of Arabia remained the domain of Semitic nomadic tribes. These hardy and fiercely independent peoples, known as the Bedouin, were arguably the greatest horse breeders of all time and gave the world the horse known today as the Arabian.

Much of the credit for the Bedouins' ability to survive in their harsh environment must be given to the camel, which provided transportation,

milk, meat, and leather and was uniquely adapted for life in the desert. Horses, on the other hand, were a luxury and relative rarity. Yet for the type of surprise skirmishes that were the hallmark of Bedouin warfare and raiding, there could be no greater advantage than to be mounted on a fleet, enduring, and courageous Arabian horse. Victory meant capturing livestock, and livestock meant survival as well as wealth for the Bedouins. Mares were preferred to stallions, likely because they were quieter and less apt to announce their presence with neighing. Their keen hearing and eyesight were also an advantage in alerting a tribe to the presence of intruders.

In exchange for the horses' importance to Bedouin life, they were treated as friends and family members. Reared lovingly by the women and children of the tribe, the Arabian horses responded to the Bedouins with the loyalty and devotion usually accorded only to their own kind. The Bedouins jealously guarded the purity of their horses, observing that judicious breeding was the key to maintaining the physical attributes and character required of their mounts.

An Arabian stallion appears as though running through the mists of time.

The Bedouins of the Najd region had a saying that proclaimed it is better to breed a mare to an average well-bred stallion than to a beautiful stallion of questionable lineage. They asserted that the offspring of the latter would become worse and worse, while the descendants of the former would continually improve. Even if a horse was taken as booty in a raid, a code of honor required that the pedigree be given to the new owner. According to the Bedouins, "A gold jewel cannot be made except from gold."

The nomadic lifestyle of the Bedouins resulted in an oral culture of stories, poetry, and genealogy, and horses were a common subject. The central themes surrounding the Arabian horse are repeated again and again—the importance of purity, nobility, bravery, beauty, and stamina. During the pre-Islamic era known as the Golden Age of Poetry, the greatest poems were purportedly inked in gold and suspended inside the temple of the holy city of Mecca. Many of these poems contained elaborate tributes to the poet's horse or camel. Imru' al-Qays, considered by many to be the greatest poet of this time period, described the attributes of his stallion:

Well-bred was he, long-bodied, outstripping
the wild beasts in speed,
Swift to attack, to flee, to turn, yet firm
as a rock swept down by the torrent,
Bay-coloured, and so smooth the saddle
slips from him, as the rain from a
smooth stone.[4]

The Golden Ode of the Arab poet Labid paid tribute to a fleet and courageous mare:

And I came down riding, my mare's neck
held loftily
as a palm fruit-laden: woe to the gatherer!
Swift was she . . . galloped she how
wrathfully . . .
Thrusteth her neck forward, shaketh her
reins galloping;
flieth as the doves fly bound for the
water-springs.[5]

The characteristics of the horses described in pre-Islamic poetry provide ample evidence that by this period the Arabian horse had become a true breed, ideally adapted to its environment and carefully bred by the Bedouins to posses the attributes of the ultimate desert warhorse.

6

The Rise of Islam

From the time of the revelations of the Prophet Muhammad, the Arabian horse was inextricably linked with the religion of Islam. The Prophet, as the foremost lover of horses in Islam, told his followers, "Take upon you the mares! Their backs are a sanctuary and their wombs are a treasure." By example, he taught his followers to honor and respect the horse. While braiding the forelock of his mare between his fingers he was heard to say, "Blessings are bound to the forelocks of horses until the Day of Judgment."

The Holy Qur'an also makes reference to the valiant Arabian warhorse in Sura 100:

> *By the steeds that run*
> *With panting breath*
> *And strike sparks of fire,*
> *And push home the charge in the morning,*
> *And raise the dust in clouds the while,*
> *And penetrate forthwith into the midst of*
>   *the foe*
> *Truly man is, to his Lord, ungrateful.*[6]

As the religion of Islam spread beyond the Arabian Peninsula, the Muslims were consistently victorious on their small and hardy horses. While their foes often considered their own mounts merely beasts of burden, the Muslims fervently believed their horses were rational beings whose hearts and minds reflected those of their riders. Two-thirds of the known world, from China to Austria, were conquered on the backs of Arabian horses.

The Islamic Dynasties of Egypt and the Arabian Horse

Under the banner of Islam, Egypt was again changed forever by the horse. The conquest of Egypt beginning in 639 CE was the first campaign in Islamic history that consisted of cavalry as the primary force.[7] Abd al-Rahman ibn Ziyad began his account of the Muslims first entering Egypt with thankfulness that they found good pasture for their horses. The acclaimed dynasties of great horsemen that followed illustrate how eagerly the Egyptians embraced the philosophies of their conquerors in regard to horses, and the Arabian became an integral element in this complex era of Egyptian history.

Egypt remained under Muslim governors from a succession of Islamic caliphates for nearly one thousand years. From 661 to 750 CE, the Ummayads, based in Damascus, successfully ruled Egypt while expanding the Islamic empire from Spain

to Asia. Continued conflict between two groups of Muslims, the Sunnis and the Shi'a, led to the downfall of the Ummayads, and during the next century the Baghdad-based Abbasid caliphate ruled Egypt.

Literature from this period indicates that Arabian horses remained essential to Muslim life. The renowned Abbasid poet al-Mutanabbi wrote:

> Fine steeds, like true friends are few,
>   even if in the eye of the inexperienced they
>   are many.
> If you have seen nothing but the beauty of
>   their markings and limbs,
> their true beauty is hidden from you.[8]

A ninth-century work from the early Abbasid period, *Kitab al-furusiya wa-l-baytara*, written by Ibn Akhi Hizam, contains detailed instructions on the care and training of horses.[9] In all instances, Ibn Akhi Hizam's primary focus was that the trainer act gently and with great care toward his mount. He also specifies different methods and equipment to be used for purebred Arabians, because of their greater sensitivity, than for mixed breeds of horses.

Balance was the keystone of his approach to riding and training, and he is quick to blame almost all vices of the horse on a bad education and not on their intrinsic nature.

Ahmad ibn Tulun, originally sent by the Abbasids to be governor of Egypt, founded the Tulunid dynasty (868–905 CE) by establishing himself as an independent ruler of the country. The importance of horses during his rule is suggested by his consideration for them when constructing one of the greatest mosques in all of Islamic architecture, the mosque of Ibn Tulun. The graceful arches that surround its vast interior courtyard convey a sense of tranquility, but the mosque compound was also built to house the honored steeds of the cavalry. Upon Ibn Tulun's death, Egypt fell once more to outside rule, this time under the Fatimids (909–1171 CE), a kingdom of rulers who claimed descent from the Prophet Muhammad's daughter Fatima.

Under the Fatimids, Arabian horses were an important symbol of wealth, generosity, and honor. When the Caliph al-Mu'izz li-Din Allah entered Egypt in 973 CE, for example, it is said that he gave a dramatic speech at Alexandria, proclaiming that

The powerful, animated movement of this young stallion is an attribute of biomechanics that a breeder attempts to imprint on the animals in his stable. Typically, the hindquarters propel the body high and forward, while the shoulders engage the front legs to cover ground.

he had come to Egypt not to increase his own wealth or importance but to maintain the true faith. He then presented a lavishly adorned horse to each of the Egyptian dignitaries who were present. Then, when the caliph entered Cairo for his first public appearance, his generosity was reciprocated by the nobles there. In *History of Egypt in the Middle Ages*, published in London in 1901, Stanley Lane-Poole wrote that the caliph's gifts included "500 horses with saddles and bridles encrusted with gold, amber and precious stones; tents of silk and cloth of gold, borne on Bactrian camels; dromedaries, mules, and camels of burden; filigree coffers full of gold and silver vessels; gold-mounted swords; caskets of chased silver containing precious stones; a turban set with jewels; and 900 boxes filled with samples of all the goods that Egypt produced." It is interesting to note that the gift of the horses heads the list.

The Arabian horse was equally important to Egypt during the Ayyubid caliphate (1171–1341 CE), founded by the great Salah al-Din al-Ayyubi (Saladin), first successor to the Fatimids. This brilliant leader valiantly defended the region against the Crusaders, driving them from Jerusalem in 1187 CE. During this conflict the knights of western Europe first encountered the swift and beautiful Arabian horse and later exported them to their home countries.

Until Egypt fell to the Ottomans in 1517 CE, a succession of Mamluk sultans ruled Egypt in two distinct dynasties, the Bahri Mamluks and the Burji Mamluks. Despite their propensity for violence and bloody struggles for power, these solider–slaves of primarily Greek, Armenian, or Russian extraction ensured the prosperity of Cairo and created the only great Egyptian empire since the age of the pharaohs. During the centuries that the Mamluks ruled, their Arabian horses were adorned in unimaginable grandeur, rivaled only by the beauty of the horses themselves. The processions of Sultan Baybars are a legendary example.[10] Streets were lined with the finest oriental rugs and sprinkled with sugared almonds to be broken apart by the hooves of the Sultan's steeds as treats for the spectators. Drifting on the breeze, the notes of a flute signaled the approach of a musician on horseback followed by an entourage of riders mounted on bejeweled Arabians, flags of the Sultan held high. Matching stallions, with saddle and bridles of exquisite ornamentation announced the arrival of the Sultan himself, turbaned and wrapped in black silk edged in gold, riding his own magnificent mount. Led horses of equal

10

splendor followed his prancing stallion, bringing to mind the words used to describe the horses of King Solomon centuries earlier: "There was no precedence for their magnificence."[11]

The second dynasty of the Mamluks, the Burji, gained control over Egypt in 1382 CE under Sultan Barquq and remained in power until the Ottoman Empire conquered Egypt in 1517 CE. Yet even after their defeat by the Ottomans, the Mamluks managed to share in the rule and wealth of Egypt, continuing their struggle to regain independence. Literature and art during these centuries of Mamluk governance reflect a devotion to Arabian horses, despite more than a few Mamluks of Mongol origin introducing the concept of the horse as gourmet fare for their lavish banquets. Numerous treatises elaborated the principles of *furusiya*, or horsemanship, which was elevated to an art form in this era, with the Arabian horse described as the finest instrument of defense. Much was also written on the game of polo, which reached its apogee during the Mamluk period.

By the time Napoleon Bonaparte arrived in 1798, the twenty thousand Mamluks in Egypt enjoyed virtual independence from the Ottomans. From the French accounts of the Egyptian invasion, it is difficult to ascertain whether Napoleon most admired the Pyramids or the grandeur of the Mamluk horsemen and their Arabian steeds. Historian Adolphe Thiers related that when the French army came upon "the gigantic Pyramids gilded by the sun," Napoleon, his face "beaming with enthusiasm," galloped ahead of his soldiers and pointing at the monuments proclaimed, "Consider that from the summits of these Pyramids forty centuries have their eyes fixed upon you." Yet his admiration of the Mamluk horsemen and their magnificent trappings was so great he adorned his own Arabian horse in their fashion and even formed his own Mamluk corps in the early nineteenth century, the last known Mamluk force.

Egypt and Arabia

The next epoch of Egyptian history was led by Muhammad Ali the Great (1769–1849). The reign of this pasha had a lasting impact on the history of Arabian horses and provides an important thread of continuity with the Egyptian Arabian horses of the present day. Muhammad Ali, an Albanian by birth, was named Pasha of Egypt by the Ottoman government in Istanbul, which gave him the governorship of the country. Muhammad Ali instituted a series of sweeping changes in agriculture, the arts and sciences, education, civil administration, and the military in an attempt to match the emerging industrial nations of modern Europe. These changes profoundly altered the course of Egypt and Egyptian society.

First, though, fearing the power of the remaining Mamluks, Muhammad Ali cleverly engineered their demise at a lavish fantasia held at his palace at the Citadel in Cairo. The Mamluk leaders accepted the pasha's invitation with enthusiasm. They were confident of their reception, as Muhammad Ali had aligned himself with them on more than one occasion on his way to becoming Pasha of Egypt. Accounts of the event vary, with some saying there were only sixty-four Mamluk leaders present, while others maintain there were nearly seven hundred. Yet in most accounts a valiant Arabian horse emerges as a savior. After the Mamluks enjoyed the hospitality of the pasha, the gates of the Citadel slammed shut suddenly behind them. Trapped, they were brutally attacked from above. One story says that once they realized their doom, the Mamluks dismounted, bravely bowed their heads, and awaited their fate. But the most widespread legend proclaims that a single Mamluk, Amin Bey, reacted in an instant, asking the ultimate sacrifice of his loyal Arabian horse. He leaped astride, galloped up the steep rampart, and commanded his stallion to leap over the great wall. The stallion obeyed without hesitation, and although the fall of forty feet proved fatal to the horse, Amin Bey became the sole survivor of the massacre.

The governance of Egypt was not the only challenge faced by Muhammad Ali. In Arabia, the amirs of the al-Saud family were becoming strong enough to worry the Ottoman rulers in Istanbul, and they looked to Muhammad Ali to ensure Ottoman control of the holy cities of Mecca and Medina. The subsequent clash between Muhammad Ali and the al-Saud had enormous importance for the Arabian breed.

The al-Saud had joined forces with the religious leader Shaykh Muhammad ibn Abd al-Wahhab (1703–92) to spread a message of pure monotheism and austerity of faith in Islam. When their armies threatened Ottoman control of the holy cities, Muhammad Ali was called upon to suppress their advances. A passion for obtaining the choicest steeds of the desert was an inadvertent outcome of his battles for control of Arabia. While Saud ibn Abd al-Aziz managed to thwart the initial Ottoman advances, his death in 1814 CE meant the loss of the al-Saud's most skillful military leader. Saud's son Abdullah, fearing defeat by the armies of Muhammad Ali's son Tusun Pasha (1794–1816), negotiated a truce that included the gift of more than two hundred of Arabia's most precious horses. After Tusun died, another of Muhammad Ali's sons, Ibrahim Pasha (1789–1848), acted as Muhammad Ali's commander and returned to Arabia to continue the battle.

When Ibrahim Pasha succeeded in capturing the al-Saud capital of Diriya in 1818, the spoils of war included the fabled Arabian horses of Najd, said to be the finest in the world. Although few of these horses were destined to reach Egypt, they made a profound impression on Ibrahim, who also came to admire the culture of the Arabs themselves. Yet before long, many of the prized horses of Arabia did arrive in Cairo. While Abdullah ibn Saud was sent to Istanbul and beheaded, despite promises that his life would be spared, his son Turki attempted to reconcile himself to the rule of the Ottomans. To satisfy Muhammad Ali's insatiable desire for purebred Arabian horses Turki sent several shipments to Egypt. By this time the ornate stables of Muhammad Ali were said to be more elaborate than his own palace. The pasha was determined to collect the best horses through any means available, including imprisonment and torture of owners who refused to sell their prized animals.

Upon the death of Turki, Faisal ibn Turki (1785–1865) rose to power with a determination to avenge the plunder of his father's land. W.G. Palgrave, who visited Faisal's stud in the Najd region of Arabia, testified to the quality of his horses by writing, "Never had I seen or imagined so lovely a collection. . . . Their appearance justified all reputation, all value, all poetry." Known as one of the greatest leaders in Saudi history, Faisal was eventually taken to Egypt to be imprisoned in the Citadel, and the circumstances of his confinement greatly influenced the future of Egyptian Arabian horses.

The Stud of Abbas Pasha I and Its Legacy

The captive Faisal ibn Turki formed a friendship with Abbas Pasha I (1813–54), Muhammad Ali's grandson, although how this relationship came to pass is not known. Abbas Pasha I is thought to have assisted in Faisal ibn Turki's eventual escape, thereby gaining Faisal's enduring gratitude. Abbas Pasha I, like Ibrahim Pasha before him, admired the Arab peoples greatly, even living among the Ruala Bedouin for a time. With Faisal's assistance, Abbas Pasha I was able to obtain many of the greatest horses in the Arabian desert. He also sent emissaries to gather an extensive history of these horses,

meticulously recording their strains and stories from the Bedouin tribes. Known as the *Abbas Pasha Manuscript*, the work remains an invaluable resource on the history of the Arabian breed. Although Abbas Pasha I is considered by some to be a failure during his tenure as Viceroy of Egypt, his dedication to the Arabian horse culminated in a collection that was perhaps the greatest the world has ever known. Countless artists were inspired by his horses' magnificence, and their works ensured that these fabled horses became a standard of classic beauty for the breed.

After Abbas Pasha was assassinated in 1854, his stud was disbanded by his heirs with heartless disregard for what he had achieved. While some members of European royalty obtained prized stock, the finest horses in the collection stayed in Egypt under the ownership of Ali Pasha Sharif. Influential in various positions of Egyptian government during the reign of the Khedive Muhammad Tawfiq, Ali Pasha Sharif also had a connection to Arabia; his father had served as governor there under Muhammad Ali. Devoting much of his life to the Arabian horse, Ali Pasha Sharif maintained a magnificent stud in Cairo. Having obtained some forty horses from the dispersal of the stud of Abbas Pasha I, he also imported numerous horses from the desert and eventually owned more than four hundred superb purebred Arabians.

When the stud of Ali Pasha Sharif was eventually dispersed, there were a number of breeders who were beneficiaries. Lady Anne Blunt, the renowned Arabist, who, along with her husband Wilfrid Scawen Blunt, had made numerous trips to the desert in search of Arabian horses, was among those fortunate to obtain stock from this stud. The Blunts wrote of the sale in a letter dated 18 January 1897:

> *The last remnants of the once celebrated stud of Ali Pasha Sherif at Cairo have just been dispersed. . . . This unique stud traced its origins to that famous collection of pure Arab mares and horses made by Abbas I, Viceroy of Egypt some 50 years ago, to obtain which he ransacked the desert of Arabia and broke down by the enormous prices he offered, the traditional refusal of the Bedouin breeders to part with their best mares.*[12]

During the late nineteenth and early twentieth centuries, several other members of the Egyptian royal family collected and bred purebred Arabian horses, and many of these bloodlines may be found in Egyptian Arabians today. The Khedive Abbas Pasha Hilmi II (1874–1914) maintained a stable of fine Arabian horses, many of which were from the stud of Ali Pasha Sharif. Prince Ahmad Pasha Kamal (1857–1907) was another famous Egyptian breeder, as was his son, Prince Yusuf Kamal. These princes, along with other breeders of the time, often received gifts of horses from various shaykhs in Arabia as well as continuing the bloodlines of horses of their Egyptian predecessors.

Prince Kamal al-Din (1874–1932) bred many Arabian horses that live on in modern pedigrees. He declined his ancestral claim to the throne, preferring his equestrian and other pursuits to governing his country, but donated several prominent horses to the government stud. Prince Muhammad Ali Tawfiq (1875–1955), twice first in line for the Egyptian throne, also never ruled his country, but he had a lasting impact on Egyptian Arabian horse breeding, maintaining four stables, the most famous of which was located at his spectacular Manyal Palace on the isle of Roda in Cairo. An extremely cultured and well-educated man, he was the author of the esteemed reference book *Breeding of Purebred Arab Horses*, published in Egypt in two volumes in the mid-1930s.

In addition to Egyptian royalty, many other prominent families in Egypt began a tradition of breeding fine Arabian horses during this time, some of whom have continued breeding until the present day. The Tahawi, a Bedouin tribe in Egypt that claims descent from the Bedouins of Arabia, were also dedicated breeders, and many private and royal stud farms in Egypt acquired horses from them over the years.

The Royal and Government Studs of Egypt

A pivotal point in Egyptian Arabian history occurred at the beginning of the twentieth century, when a program was instituted to manage the breeding of purebred horses in Egypt. Founded in 1908 under the patronage of King Fuad, the Royal Agricultural Society (RAS) obtained most of its original bloodstock through the generosity of the royal families of Egypt, including many horses from the breeders previously mentioned. Of particular significance is that a large number of the foundation horses for the RAS descended from the celebrated horses of Abbas Pasha I and Ali Pasha Sharif, thus ensuring that this valuable blood bred on into future generations. The RAS maintained two farms, Bahtim and Kafr Farouk, until 1930 when all of the horses were moved to Kafr Farouk, the larger facility.

17

Part of the mission of the RAS was to ensure a source of horses suitable for the military and police, and stallions were often sent to the provinces in order to upgrade local stock. A succession of capable veterinarians from Egypt and abroad managed the stud, and a system of herdbooks was put in place, becoming valuable references for future students of the breed.

The royal stables of kings Fuad and Farouk, named the Inshass Stud, after its location northeast of Cairo, maintained approximately one hundred fifty Arabian horses. King Fuad was a great enthusiast of horse racing, and his son, King Farouk, was a great collector of many fine things, including Arabian horses. Several important mares at the stud were gifts from King Ibn Saud of Saudi Arabia, while the majority came from the bloodstock of Prince Kamal al-Din, Prince Muhammad Ali Tawfiq, and the horses of the RAS. After the revolutionary government seized power in 1952, the horses of the Inshass Stud were auctioned off and many were lost to the breed. Fortunately, several important stallions and broodmares were incorporated into the breeding program of the RAS, which was renamed the Egyptian Agricultural Organization (EAO) under the new government, and the

name of the farm also changed from Kafr Farouk to El Zahraa.

In the decade that followed the change in government, the fate of the Egyptian Arabian horse was uncertain. Because of changes in laws to limit personal assets, many of the private breeders were forced to disperse their horses. At one point it was also decided that the Arabian horses of the EAO were a symbol of past wealth and excess and that the stud should be eliminated. The then minister of agriculture, Dr. Sayed Marei, made an impassioned plea that the horses had to be saved. "It will be as if we are erasing the Great Pyramids of Egypt," he commented of the proposed action. His words were heeded, and the EAO remained the government stud. In the ensuing decades, breeders from around the world came to know the beautiful palm-lined entrance and eucalyptus-shaded paddocks of El Zahraa, as the EAO became a source of important bloodstock that changed the face of Arabian horse breeding worldwide and ensured that the Egyptian Arabian became the most prized of all Arabian horses. Today the EAO is thriving and is home to several hundred horses. The organization serves as the official registrar of all Arabian horses in Egypt and also publishes the official studbook and supervises private stud farms, including the identification, exportation, and importation of Arabian horses.

The Egyptian Arabian Horses of Today

To understand why the Egyptian Arabian holds such an exalted position in the world of Arabian horses, it is necessary to turn again to Arabia and their other desert homelands. By the mid-twentieth century the advent of mechanization meant that the horse had been replaced as the ideal vehicle of desert warfare. The traditional way of life of the Bedouin was fast disappearing and this development had a devastating influence on the number and quality of horses being bred. For centuries Europeans had traveled to the desert in search of fine Arabian horses, exporting hundreds to improve their native breeds and to maintain purebred breeding at various royal and state studs. And Egypt, largely because of the importations resulting from Muhammad Ali's earlier conflict with Arabia, had become a repository for the finest remaining Arabians of pure desert descent. Of equal importance is that astute breeders, first at the stables of Egyptian royal and prominent families and later at the RAS and EAO, had carefully bred these horses to retain their superior qualities. In an ironic twist of fate,

Egypt, where the first known depictions of Arabian-type horses were found thousands of years ago, had become the modern source for the classic Arabian horse.

In the late 1950s and throughout the 1960s and 1970s, breeders around the world increasingly began to look to Egypt for exceptional Arabian horses to serve as foundation stock. The resulting exportations, particularly to the United States and Europe, had a profound impact on breeders there. European state studs, such as Marbach in Germany and Babolna in Hungary, began programs concentrating on Egyptian bloodlines. Appreciated for their distinct elegance and type, the Egyptian horses also earned countless championships in the show ring, furthering their popularity. In 1969, a breeders' organization in the United States, the Pyramid Society, was formed to ensure the preservation and perpetuation of these unique bloodlines. Referring to the horses as "straight" Egyptians, meaning that they descended exclusively from horses bred from specific Egyptian bloodlines, this organization was instrumental in uniting breeders passionate about these horses. Today almost every country in the world that breeds Arabians has stud farms devoted exclusively to the Egyptian Arabian.

These horses have enjoyed astounding success in the show ring, considering their rarity. At the most prestigious Arabian shows in the last few decades, such as the world championships at the Salon du Cheval in Paris or the Nations Cup in Aachen, Germany, it is not unusual for many of the champions to be Egyptian Arabians. The use of Egyptian blood in other Arabian horses has also been a proven formula for successful breeding, and at a recent world championship, every single champion boasted a sire line tracing to an Egyptian Arabian. Even prestigious historical studs renowned for their own bloodlines, such as Janów Podlaski and Michałów of Poland, have introduced Egyptian blood to their herds.

A further testament to the importance of the Egyptian Arabian is the renaissance of Arabian horse breeding taking place in the Arabian Gulf countries. Understanding that the Arabian horse is a vital part of their cultural heritage, far-sighted breeders began seeking horses that would once again ensure that the Arabian Peninsula was home to the best Arabian bloodlines. An overwhelming majority of these breeders turned to the Egyptian Arabian to provide their foundation bloodstock, recognizing that these horses were the world's best remaining source of pure desert blood.

In addition to the horses bred by the EAO, the private breeders of Egypt must be given considerable credit for developing world-class breeding programs that have produced exceptional Egyptian Arabians, including world champions. In recent years there has been an explosion of enthusiastic new breeders in Egypt, numbering in the hundreds, and the Egyptian Arabian is thriving in its homeland.

Egyptian Arabians share the distinguishing characteristics common to all Arabian horses: beautiful heads, triangular in shape, often dished, with a small muzzle, large dark eyes, and flaring nostrils that 'drink' the desert wind; arched necks and short backs, often possessing fewer lumbar vertebrae than other horses; well-sprung ribs and deep chests allowing for strength and stamina to cover long distances; proudly carried tails, held aloft like a flag and thought to help dissipate body heat when a horse is galloping in the blazing heat of the desert; fine, dense bone; round, flinty hooves;

The intelligent, knowing eye of the Arabian horse that has carried its rider and generations of warriors to victory through many wars.

20

and smooth, rounded bodies with strong coupling and a flat croup. Yet Egyptian Arabians seem to have an overabundance of these characteristics combined with a unique elegance and refinement that sets them apart from Arabian horses of other bloodlines. Although difficult to define in words, there is an unmistakable 'desert' look to the Egyptian Arabian. The skin is exceptionally fine, meaning that the veins, bones, and tendons are easily visible, giving a sculptural appearance to the horse, often referred to as 'dryness.' This unique look is reminiscent of the horses depicted by the famous orientalist painters of centuries past, whose inspiration included both the fabled horses of Najd and those of Abbas Pasha I.

The significance of Egyptian Arabians being bred and raised in a country with an environment similar to their homelands cannot be ignored. Only a few generations away from their desert ancestors, they continue to have sand beneath their hooves and breathe the desert air. While the historic studs of Europe and the Americas have bred influential Arabian horses for centuries, most are many generations away from their desert forebears, and the lush green pastures and hospitable climates where they live are a stark contrast to the home environment of the breed. There is no doubt that these conditions have had some effect over time on the appearance of the horses. Breed selection is another factor. From the era of the Islamic conquest, Arabians horses have had a constant presence in Egypt, ensuring that breeders have been highly attuned to the authentic characteristics of the breed. In other countries where Arabians were originally imported to improve cavalry horses, the influence of domestic breeds is sometimes visible in breeding selections, whether inadvertent or intentional.

Like all Arabian horses, the Egyptian Arabian is renowned for its unique character, a product of the way these horses were raised for centuries by their Bedouin breeders. They exhibit a closeness to their human companions unrivaled in any other horse. Yet more than horses from many other Arabian bloodlines, the Egyptian Arabian exhibits a unique sensitivity. These horses do not tolerate abuse in any form and seem more attuned to the actions and feelings of their owners than other Arabian horses. Fiery and proud, Egyptian Arabians are nevertheless loyal, gentle, and willing when treated with the respect and honor they deserve.

It is often said that Arabians are the most beautiful horses and the Arabian horses of Egypt are the most beautiful Arabians. Throughout history, a succession of visionary breeders, often facing great challenges, has preserved and protected these splendid animals. An enduring symbol of beauty and nobility, they are Egypt's gift to the world.

God has gifted man with coursers of the highest breeding . . . . He made horses the most beautiful means of riding, the beauty of pageants, the most splendid gifts, and the most desirable possessions . . . .
—From the seventeenth-century manuscript of Shaykh Muhammad al-Bakhsi al-Halabi

1 The Kikkuli tablets, in the collections of the Vorder-asiatisches Museum in Berlin, are named after one of the authors of these five cuneiform tablets. Thought to have been composed by Hurrian-Mittani experts, the tablets are a detailed training manual for chariot horses and include instructions for exercise, conditioning, feeding, harnessing, and veterinary care. For further information see Joachim Marzahn, "Training Instructions for Horses from Cuneiform Texts: The Kikkuli Tablets and Related Material from the Vorderasiastiches Museum in Berlin," in David Alexander, ed., *Furusiyya*, vol. 1 (Riyadh, 1996).

2 Eva March Tappan, ed., *The World's Story: A History of the World in Story, Song and Art, Vol. III: Egypt, Africa, and Arabia*, trans. W.K. Flinders Petrie (Boston, 1914).

3 There is still considerable controversy as to when the horse arrived in the Arabian Peninsula. The rock art that depicts equines is also difficult to date precisely. Several illustrations of this rock art, as well as an overview of horses in pre-Islamic Arabia, are found in M.C.A. McDonald's article, "Hunting, Fighting and Raiding: The Horse in Pre-Islamic Arabia," *Furusiyya*, vol. 1.

4 A.J. Arberry, *The Seven Odes* (London, 1957).

5 Lady Anne Blunt and Wilfrid S. Blunt, trans. *The Seven Golden Odes of Pagan Arabia: known also as the Moallakat* (London, 1903).

6 Abdullah Yusuf Ali, *The Holy Qur'an: text, translation and commentary* (New York, 1998).

7 An overview of the military history of the Muslim conquest of Egypt may be found in *Armies of the Muslim Conquest* by David Nicolle (Oxford, 1993).

8 A.J. Arberry, *Poems of Al Mutanabbi* (London, 1967).

9 Beate Siewart-Mayer, "Riding in the Early Abbasid Period," *Furusiyya*, vol. 1.

10 For further reading on the horses of Sultan Baybars see Judith Forbis, *The Classic Arabian Horse* (New York, 1976). This book is also a superb reference on the history of Egyptian Arabian horses.

11 From the fourteenth-century manuscript, *Hilyat al-fursan wa shi'ar al-shuj'an* by Ali ibn Abd al-Rahman ibn Hudhayl al-Andalusi, translated by C. Culbertson.

12 This letter addressed to *The Times* is referenced in several books; however, sources disagree as to whether it was penned by Lady Anne Blunt or Wilfrid Blunt.

PHOTOGRAPHING THE ARABIAN HORSE

Nasr Marei

When you look at a photograph of an Arabian horse you are not merely looking at that specific horse; you are also looking at the history of everything that has contributed to its existence in today's world. Centuries of dramatic and widespread events have shaped its conformation and persona. The Arabian horse has, foremost throughout its history, been a weapon in brutally fought wars in the harshest conditions of survival: environments with little shelter, food, or water. For thousands of years, the horse had to eke out its existence in the cruel, unforgiving terrain of the Najd Desert of Saudi Arabia, a land of great extremes and hardship. The area can almost instantly transform from blistering heat to biting cold as the sun plummets over the horizon.

A substantial part of the beauty of the Arabian horse is its utility. Its refined beauty can seem a contradiction to the hardiness of the breed. However, you cannot separate its overall appearance from its adaptability and survival skills. In order to stay alive as a warhorse it had to develop tremendous endurance as well as agility and a striking ability to understand the demands and wishes of its

Majesty, elegance, and focus are epitomized by this Egyptian stallion at the peak of his powers.

25

rider, who had to focus all of his concentration on the battle. The enduring bond between horse and rider is evident in the strong companionship that is celebrated in Arab literature and in stories from today's stables. Its courage is legendary. Soundness of limb and adaptability in spite of deprivation brought on by lack of food and water, as well as the hardship of punishing terrain, were necessary for its very existence.

Even though it is almost impossible to capture the true essence of the Arabian horse, I have tried through the years to do just that. I hope that you can enjoy these images and feel something of what so many devoted breeders, horse lovers, and artists have attempted to do before me. The photographs are divided into groupings for convenience, however they all form the quintessential creature that is the Arabian horse.

The magic bond between a mare and her foal illustrates the wisdom, love, and care that can also form the relationship with her owner.

26

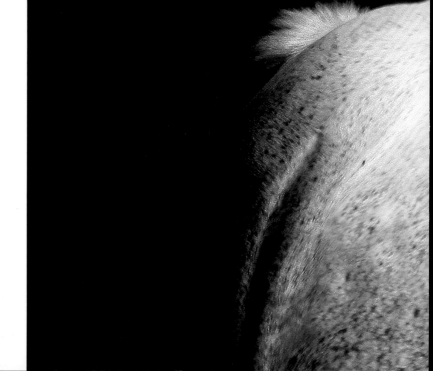

TYPE: THE IDEAL ARABIAN HORSE

Everything that we have read until now factors into the development of what is referred to as the unique 'type' of the Arabian horse. Even though we address different elements of conformation and character, they must actually be viewed as part of the complete picture. You cannot consider any one element as the most essential. They all must complement and reinforce each other in order to have unity and symmetry. Type is difficult to define in exact terms. It is a combination of everything that makes the Arabian horse unique: elegance, refinement, power, strong flowing movement, chiseled head, balance, and great presence. These are the qualities, which, thus presented, insist that you look at an Arabian horse and give it the respect that it demands.

There are differences in conformation and attitude between mares and stallions that often manifest from an early age as the foals begin to display their sense of self. You can observe the foal developing through its early years into adolescence and maturity while constantly improving on its earliest characteristics. The mares should always have a feminine manner and appearance. They are a bit more refined than the males, with a gentleness and soft expression. The neck should be lighter and flexible in order to be able to reach down and help the foal to nurse. Even though they have the wonderful fluidity of motion, pride, and elegance of the breed, they usually display power with an extra touch of grace and lightness not seen in stallions.

When an Arabian stallion is in full performance mode, there is no mistaking his masculinity. The words that best describe him are a commanding presence, unleashed power, and unassailable pride. His neck is heavier than the mare's and he has a more dominant crest. The muscles of the haunches are clearly visible, accentuating the strength of his movement.

... *her noble endurance and her impetuosity ...*
carry her to the front of the dash of the galloping steeds ...
When she has been fined down by training, she is like a young gazelle ...
With her muscles and upper parts firmly knit,
And her lower limbs made nimble and light ...

From the *Muzarrid* of Yazid, seventh century

The pre-potent Arabian type as it evolves from a week-old foal into a two-year-old filly, showing the refinement that must be present from birth.

The elegance and grace
that remain consistent
from birth into early
maturity, as exemplified
by a two-week-old filly,
a young mare, and a
four-year-old mare

The power and masculinity of a male Arabian manifest throughout early maturity as seen in one- to three-year-old stallions.

The Arabian horse, having been originally created out of the wind, reflects the supremacy of the element of air over the other three elements of nature: fire, earth, and water . . .

From the seventeenth-century manuscript of
Shaykh Muhammad al-Bakhsi al-Halabi

41

*I was convinced that Phili was a horse for
heroes and gods, and I treated him accordingly.
He stood his honors well . . . .*

Carl R. Raswan, *Drinkers of the Wind*

Power masked by deceptive fragility. The fineness of bones and skin deceive the observer by concealing the tremendous strength in both mares and stallions.

CONFORMATION

Balance and fluid agility are the hallmarks of good conformation. The harmony of an Arabian must show the symmetry and proportion that determine his dexterity. The top-line of the Arabian has a level appearance, with a slight springiness that allows placement of a saddle. The back is shorter than most other breeds, which contributes to flexibility and maneuverability. An almost straight croup should lead to a high set tail, which immediately springs to life to become one of the hallmarks of an Arabian. At a walk or trot, the tail flags high over the croup in an arch like an ostrich plume and may even roll forward over the back. At the gallop and strong dramatic gaits, the tail will flare behind the horse. This is one of the major identifying characteristics of the Arabian horse.

An Arabian horse in movement will show highly defined muscle structure. Power is evident in whatever they do. Although somewhat shorter in stature than many of the European horses, they are nevertheless capable of carrying riders of substantial size, and their endurance for distance riding is legendary. This is due to the soundness and density of their bones, especially the legs, as well as their having a compact balanced center of gravity. To watch an Arabian horse appear to fly across the sand with head high, tail flagging, and eyes devouring the landscape ahead is to see some of the qualities that define the breed.

Although much is said about movement, elegance, power, and the distinctive features that make the Arabian horse a creature of great notice, it is the head that always draws us to study and understand the extraordinary dignity and character that we see. The head of the Arabian horse commands our attention. We gaze at intelligence, curiosity, and intensity as part of the special beauty that exists in no other breed.

Streaming manes and tails highlight the delicate features
of these two young fillies.

Large, round, expressive eyes, flaring nostrils, and small, gracefully shaped, well defined ears that gently point inward are set into a sculpted head. The term 'dryness' is used to describe the look of an Arabian head. As an Arabian grows from foal to adult, its skin becomes tighter over its bone structure, which gives the unique chiseled appearance that has made sculptures and paintings as dramatic and expressive as the real horse.

An Arabian head is smaller and more defined than most other breeds. Structurally, it is shorter and narrower, with a graceful curve sloping from a slightly prominent forehead down to a small squared muzzle, and the nostrils that flare with excitement or effort. However, to the artist, the breeder, and anyone who has the good fortune to be close to these horses, it is always the eyes that capture and hold full attention. They truly show the soul of this wonderful creature with its intellect, gentleness, and curiosity to know and understand everything that it sees. The Arabian horse can hold you with the force of his gaze.

Of course, the head must be viewed as a continuation of the curve and placement of the neck in completing the look of the horse. The neck should be graceful, slender, clean-cut where it connects to the head—and flexible, with stallions having a broader and more powerful neck than mares to convey their image of power; yet the neck must be in proportion to the rest of the body. It is always a mark of the passion of the stallion to display the dramatically arched neck when he is showing himself off to an audience or to other horses.

. . . A mare long of body, short of hair, whose spirit is unfailing.
compactly and firmly built, slender as a staff . . .
A bay, with her back strongly-knit . . . her sires have lifted
her line to the best of strains . . .

From the *Mufarrid* of Yazid, seventh century

Pride, elegance, and
character are reflected
in these Arabians' finely
sculpted heads.

62

Large, soft, round eyes,
and flaring nostrils add
to the wonder of the
Arabian horse.

65

66

Horses, to the Arabs, were the most significant thing in life; they were the symbol of their erected fortresses, their everlasting treasures, their finest glory, and their securest way of defense. As such, the Arabs took great interest in horses, and excelled in their knowledge about these animals more than all other nations.

al-Alusi, historian

Those were the classic remarks of my old Rittmeister, a captain of cavalry. "Never let his fire die out, but kindle it with words, and make him feel the joy that is within you; let him know that you are honored to be carried along on his strong shoulders and back and on his swift feet."

Carl R. Raswan, *Drinkers of the Wind*

To know the Arabian horse, one should first understand that which made him—Arabia and the Arabs.

W.R. Brown, *The Horse of the Desert*

Nobility and grace are
captured even in tranquil
moments with a gentle
curve of delicate legs.

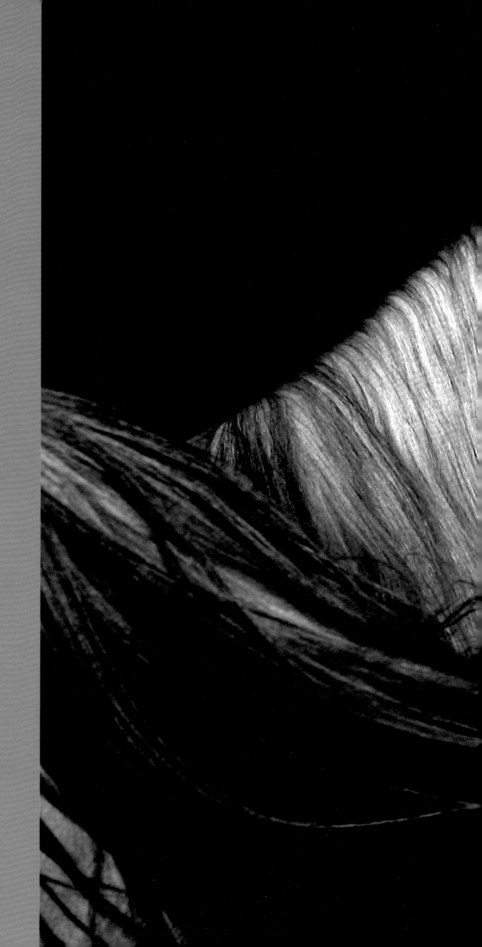

The beauty of his head, ears, eyes, jaw, mouth, and nostril should be seen to be appreciated. The ears are not so small, but are so perfectly shaped that they appear small. The head is short from the eye to the muzzle and broad and well-developed above. The eye is particularly soft and intelligent, with a sparkle characteristic of the breed. Yet when it lights up with excitement, it does not have the strained, wild look and pained, staring expression often seen in European horses. The nostrils, long and puckered, are drawn back and are capable of great distention. The neck is a model of strength and forms a perfect arch that matches the arch of his tail. The build of the Arab is perfect. It is essentially that of utility.

Homer Davenport, *My Quest of the Arabian Horse*

HARMONY
AND MOVEMENT

Conformation enables harmonious movement; a horse must have excellent conformation in order to embody the ideals that distinguish the Arabian. The entire framework and attributes of the horse come into play with movement that should be light and fluid as well as demonstrative of great power. This power emanates from the strength of the hindquarters, which propel the horse forward into the motion that flows from a well-angled shoulder. Lightness on the ground and tremendous fluidity bring gracefulness into the breathtaking movement.

Very often a person looking at horses is drawn to a particular color. While a shiny and silky coat contributes to the harmony of the complete horse, it is only one element. It is a reflection of the health and condition of the animal. The skin of an Arabian horse is notable for its fineness. In some horses it is almost transparent so that the veins are easily visible and reveal the blood running through them under any exertion. A horse in good condition will have silky lustrous hair and a fine mane and tail. The colors of Arabians are gray, chestnut, bay, and black, with the majority being gray. The predominance of the color gray stems from the need for natural protection from the harsh light of the sun. The gray color is a natural camouflage in the desert, which protects the horse from raiders and reflects damaging rays from the sun.

An Arabian foal shows
personality as well as
balance in exuberant
early playfulness.

92

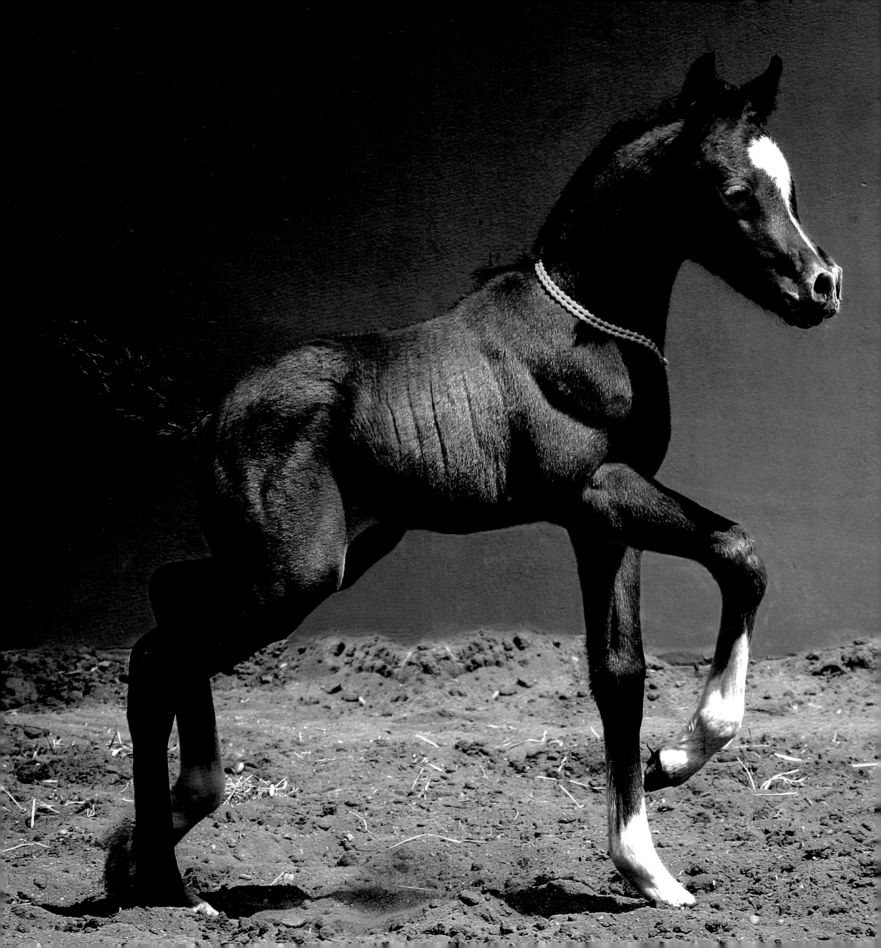

Fine bones and sturdy legs permit agility and control in all terrain. This is represented here by a month-old colt and a mature mare.

An Egyptian stallion in full motion showing the powerful arched neck that compliments the set of the shoulder. This balances the thrust of the strong hindquarters and propels the forward movement.

Two Egyptian mares, one in motion and one in repose. Both show the gentle demeanor and grace that personify the breed.

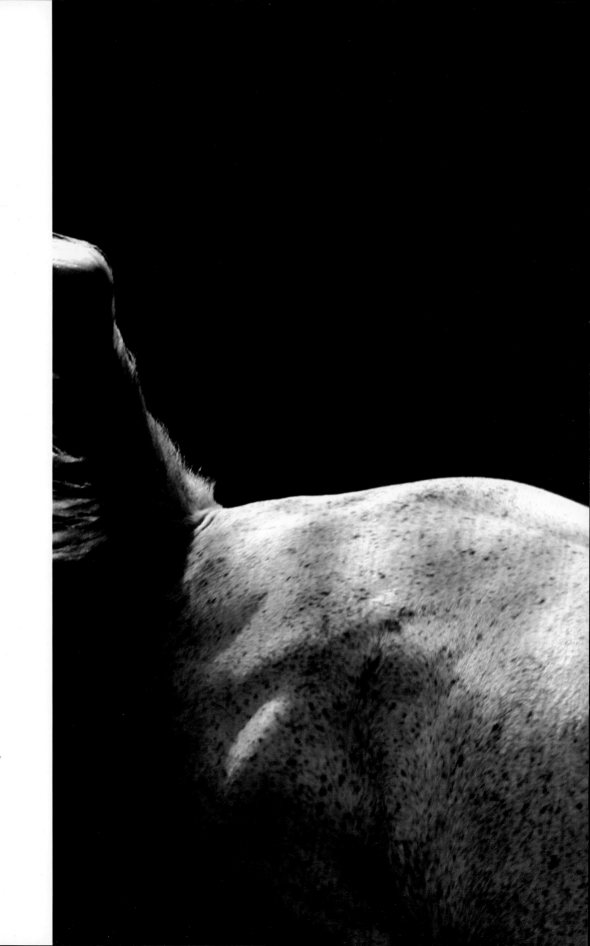

Tightly controlled energy
that can explode at will.

And many a day like the night of lovers I have
ridden through, watching the sun when it should
set, my eyes fixed on the ears of a bright-blazed
horse which was as if a star of the night remained
between its eyes . . .

al-Mutanabbi

FAMILY

The moment of birth is always magical. Mares carry the baby for eleven months and they are able to maintain their powerful movement throughout the pregnancy. As with most species they also know how to protect themselves and the unborn foal. At the time of foaling there is instant bonding as the mare cleans and dries the baby. Since foals are prey in the natural world, the job of the mother is to help the foal onto its feet as quickly as possible so that he learns how to use his legs, strengthening his chances for flight and survival.

For the time that they are together until the foal is weaned, they are inseparable. One of the greatest pleasures of breeding is to watch the mare and foal out in the paddock as the baby mirrors the mother's movements. Some youngsters show independence earlier than others and although they may prance and fly around the paddock exhibiting a great sense of self-confidence, they still stay close to the mother at the end of the romp. The dished profile is often more noticeable in the foals than in the more mature horse, with the changes prominent through their development.

It is an interesting point that all foals are born varying shades of dark brown and either stay dark or change through the years into gray. They range in color from chestnut to copper and deep silver. The bays can have a dark to medium brown body but must have the defining black mane and tail. Grays can vary from dappled charcoal to rose gray before turning white. Some of the prized grays develop into what is called 'flea-bitten,' which is the spotting of dark marks that is actually the black skin showing through the coat.

Even though the Arabian's original home
was the stark desert, the horse is adaptable
to almost any environment.

All Arabian foals are born varying shades of brown. Some may remain chestnut or bay, others will change to gray or white. Here, we see a mare with a flea-bitten coat showing dark specks through the gray. This foal will eventually have a similar coat.

In the photograph on the left the profiles show how the dam can stamp her characteristics onto her foal.

117

This three-week-old colt manifests the intelligence, pride, and physical attributes including the dished face and high tail carriage that will be developed and refined as he grows to maturity.

Even in an advanced stage of pregnancy, this mare (above) exhibits the
natural balance and agility that serves the Arabian so well in its original
habitat of the desert.

123

This mare (above) has passed the classic dry, chiseled head with the large eye, dished profile, and arched neck on to her son (right).

EPILOGUE

Throughout most of its history the Arabian horse has been the treasured possession of royalty, heads of state, and Arab shaykhs. Even today, an Arabian stallion can be a gift from a head of state to an honored guest. As we look at the photographs in this book, we can feel not only some of this history but also the magnificence of the horse itself; and while a photograph can capture the moment and provide a glimpse into the essence, it cannot replicate reality.

It is only by experiencing the purebred Arabian horse and its spectacular persona in a completely personal way that we can participate and revel in its magic. We must see, touch, inhale, and with good fortune, ride the horse. We must live with it on a day-to-day basis to more fully understand and appreciate the glory that is the Arabian horse and in this way participate in the extraordinary history that has shaped the horses as they are.

It is through seeing them free in nature that we can revel in their beauty. No matter how often we watch the Arabian horse at play in his environment, free with nature, performing to an audience, or skimming across the ground with the wind whistling past, to hear his nicker that calls to us as we walk into the barn and see the love that emanates from one companion to another is to observe the Arabian's true essence. This is what all art and poetry convey as the special character of the Arabian horse.

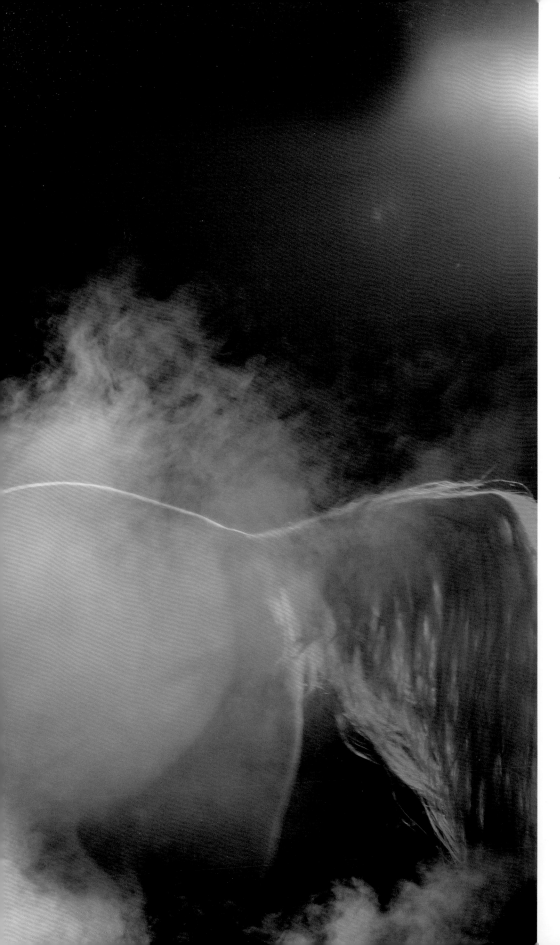

And in truth she has ever been to me a precious possession, born and brought up in our tents: of all possessions, that which has been born and bred with one's people is the most precious.

From the *Muzarrid* of Yazid, in tribute
to his mare, seventh century

131

SELECT BIBLIOGRAPHY

Alexander, David, ed. *Furusiyya*. 2 vols. Riyadh, 1996.

Ali, Abdullah Yusuf. *The Holy Qur'an: text, translation and commentary*. New York, 1998.

Ali, HH Prince Muhammad. *Breeding of Pure Bred Arab Horses*. Cairo, 1935.

al-Alusi, "Bolough Al-Arab fi Ma'rifat 'Ahwal Al-Arab," trans. Dr. Munzer A. Absi and Asmahan Sallah, in *Merit of the Horse in Islam and Sketches on Coursers of the Highest Breeding*. Aleppo, 1996.

Arberry, A.J. *Poems of Al Mutanabbi*. London, 1967.

———. *The Seven Odes*. London, 1957.

Archer, Rosemary and James Fleming, ed. *Lady Anne Blunt Journals and Correspondence 1878–1917*. Cheltenham, 1986.

Asil Club. *Asil Arabians The Noble Arabian Horses*, vol. 4. Hildesheim, 1993.

Blunt, Lady Anne. *A Pilgrimage to Nejd*. London, 1881.

Blunt, Lady Anne and Wilfrid S. Blunt, trans. *The Seven Golden Odes of Pagan Arabia: known also as the Moallakat*. London, 1903.

Brown, W.R. *The Horse of the Desert*. New York, 1929. Reprinted, Hildesheim, 1979.

Daumas, General E. *The Horses of the Sahara, and the Manners of the Desert*. London, 1863.

Davenport, Homer. *My Quest of the Arabian Horse*. London, 1911.

Al-Dumyati, Al-Hafez Abdul-Mu'men and Muhammad Al-Bakhsi Al-Halabi, *Merit of the Horse in Islam* and *Sketches on Coursers of the Highest Breeding*, trans. Dr. Munzer A. Absi and Asmahan Sallah. Aleppo, 1996. (Al-Dumyati is the author of *Merit of the Horse in Islam* and Al-Halabi is the author of *Coursers of the Highest Breeding*.)

Forbis, Judith. *Authentic Arabian Bloodstock*. Vol. 1, *A Reference Guide, Historical Articles, and Racing Records*. Mena, AR, 1990.

———. *The Classic Arabian Horse*. New York, 1976.

Guarmani, Carlo. *Northern Najd: A Journey from Jeruslem to Anaiza in Qasim*. London, 1938.

Ibn Hudhayl al-Andalusi, Ali ibn Abd al-Rahman. and *La parure des cavaliers et l'insigne des preux*. Translation of *Hilyat al-fursan wa shi'ar al-shuj'an* by Louis Mercier. Paris, 1924.

Irwin, Robert, ed. *Night and Horses and the Desert: An Anthology of Classical Arabic Literature*. New York, 2001.

Lyall, Charles James. *Translations of Ancient Arabian Poetry*. London, 1930.

Olsen, Sandra L. *Horses Through Time*. Carnegie Museum of Natural History, 1996.

Palgrave, William Gifford. *Personal Narrative of a Year's Journey through Central and Eastern Arabia (1862–1863)*, 2 vols. London, 1865.

Pearson, Colin, with Kees Mol. *The Arabian Horse Families of Egypt*. Cheltenham, 1988.

The Pyramid Society. *Reference Handbook of Straight Egyptian Horses*, vol. 9. Lexington, KY, 2006.

Raswan, Carl R. *Drinkers of the Wind*. New York, 1942.

Sherif, Gülsün and Judith Forbis. *The Abbas Pasha Manuscript: And Horses and Horsemen of Arabia and Egypt during the Time of Abbas Pasha, 1800–1860*. Mena, AR, 1993.

Tappan, Eva March, ed. *The World's Story: A History of the World in Story, Song and Art, Vol. III: Egypt, Africa, and Arabia*, trans. W.K. Flinders Petrie. Boston, 1914.

Thorau, Peter. *The Lion of Egypt: Sultan Baybars I and the Near East in the Thirteenth Century*, trans. P.M. Holt. London, 1992.

Upton, Peter. *The Arab Horse*. Manchester, 2006.

Wentworth, Judith Anne Dorothea, Lady. *The Authentic Arabian Horse*. London, 1945.

Yazid, *Muzarrid*, seventh century, in *The Mufaddaliyat: An Anthology of Ancient Arabian Odes*, trans. Sir Charles Lyall. Oxford, 1921.